Project editor: Jennifer Holder
Design: Robert Glover, Dina Sorn

Scriptures quoted from the *International Children's Bible®*,
New Century Version®, copyright © 1986, 1988, 1999 by
Tommy Nelson™, a division of Thomas Nelson, Inc.,
Nashville, Tennessee 37214. Used by permission.

ISBN 0-7847-1376-6

08 07 06 05 04 03 02   9 8 7 6 5 4 3 2 1

Presented to

_____

by

_____

on

_____

Cc

The First Christmas

The First Christmas
An ABC Book

retold by Laura Derico
illustrated by Kelly Cottrell

The **angel** said to Mary, "Fear not! You will have a **baby**.
And you will call the baby Jesus."

baby

Cc Christ

This baby would be Jesus the **Christ**, the Son of God.

Dd decree

A **decree** was sent from the king and **everyone** traveled to the cities to pay taxes.

Ee everyone

Joseph and Mary went to Bethlehem, and while they were there, the time came for the baby to be born.

The shepherds were watching their **flocks** in the fields.
An angel came and said, "Fear not! I bring you good news of
great joy! Your Savior was born today in Bethlehem!"

Hh heavenly host

Then the skies were filled with **heavenly host**, praising God. "Glory to God in the highest, and on earth peace, good will toward men."

At that time, the city of Bethlehem was very crowded because so many people had come to pay taxes.

Jj Joseph

The **inn** had no room for **Joseph** and Mary.

Kk **king**   Ll **little**

So the **King**, the **little** Lord Jesus, was born in the place
where the animals were kept. Mary wrapped the newborn
baby in swaddling clothes and laid him in a **manger**.

Mm manger

Nn **night** **Oo**

That **night**, the shepherds hurried **over** the fields to Bethlehem.

over   **Pp**   praise

They saw Jesus, and gave **praise** to God.

Qq quiet

Mary was **quiet** and thoughtful.

Rr rejoice

She listened to the shepherds **rejoice**.

A **star** shone brightly in the night sky. Men came from the east with **treasures** for the child.

treasures **Uu up**

They looked **up** and followed the star to the place where the child was.

Xx Yy exceeding joy

When the **visit** was over, the **wise men** went back to their country. They rejoiced with **exceeding** great **joy** because they had seen Jesus.

Sleep in heavenly peace.

"For unto you is born this day . . . . a Savior, which is Christ the Lord." Luke 2:11

Sleep in heavenly peace.

"For unto you is born this day . . . . a Savior, which is Christ the Lord." Luke 2:11